BERKLEE PRESS

berklee jazz guitar chord
DICTIONARY

rick peckham

edited by
jonathan feist

Berklee Press

Vice President: Dave Kusek

Dean of Continuing Education: Debbie Cavalier

Managing Editor: Jonathan Feist

Director of Business Affairs: Robert F. Green

Senior Designer: Robert Heath

Editorial Assistants: Rajasri Mallikarjuna, Jonathan Whalen

ISBN-13: 978-0-87639-079-5

1140 Boylston Street
Boston, MA 02215-3693 USA
(617) 747-2146

Visit Berklee Press Online at
www.berkleepress.com

DISTRIBUTED BY

HAL•LEONARD®
CORPORATION
7777 W. BLUEMOUND RD. P.O. BOX 13819
MILWAUKEE, WISCONSIN 53213

Visit Hal Leonard Online at
www.halleonard.com

Contents

Introduction

The *Berklee Jazz Guitar Chord Dictionary* is a resource for 7th-chord voicings and other frequently encountered jazz chord shapes on the fretboard.

The following diagrams indicate what notes you should use for each chord voicing. These chord blocks will show you the right shapes, but as a musician, you owe it to your audience and yourself to hear the music before you play it. This material will help you to map out the sounds on your fretboard. With time, you will hear the chords before you play them.

Strive to play these chords with a solid time feel, a full tone, and attacks with your "picking hand" that match the level of intensity of the music you're attempting to play.

Some tips for getting a good chord sound:

- Take special care to play the notes requested—and to *leave out*, or mute the strings with the x symbol above them. Keep the extra strings out of the sound.

- Use the edges of your fingers of your fretting hand to mute unwanted strings. Focus your strumming (or finger-picking attacks) on the indicated strings. Avoid sounding the others.

- When strumming across the strings, make the speed of your stroke fast enough to give the illusion of one simultaneous sound made up of all the chord voices.

- When you're using your fingers to pluck chords, take care to balance the level of each chord tone. A common tendency is to hit the outermost notes with the most force, resulting in a thinner texture. You're working to put those notes on the frets; make sure that the listener can hear them!

- While forming the chords, make sure that your fingers are as close to the intended frets as possible.

- When changing chords, mute the strings by lifting your fingers from the strings, but still touching them, to hold them still as you slide to the next chord.

- Make sure all notes ring. If you're not hearing all the notes clearly, keep working to curve your fingers and adjust your hand position on the intended frets to make the sound shine through your instrument.

Playing chords effectively takes time, and the learning process requires practice. There are three common stages of development.

- **Physical Stamina**: Building your hand muscles

- **Muscle Memory**: Memorizing the proper chord-voicing shapes

- **Informed Musical Instincts**: Using these chords to make music

Here are some other things to keep in mind:

- While practicing, stay vigilant, playing in time and using a metronome or drum machine. Stay with a musical task until you can make it groove with a strong time feel.

- Play with other musicians whenever possible, as often as you can. Practicing by yourself is only part of the overall plan.

- Make sure that the chords that you play fit well into your playing situation. Should your voicings contain a lot of notes or a few? Listen to the overall texture, and make a musical decision.

- Listen to the originators of the styles that you love. It's one of the best ways to keep yourself inspired—and to help you to keep the highest musical values in mind.

- Listen to great guitarists, but don't stop there. Focus on performers of other instruments as well. Bring it all together to help you to develop your own unique voice.

Keep working, and be patient with yourself. Having the physical strength and the knowledge of the shapes provide means to musical ends. With time, you'll be able to choose from a variety of options. If you keep at it, you'll definitely get there!

—Rick Peckham

PART I.
CHORDS

Chapter 1.
Moveable 7th Chord Shapes

Major 7

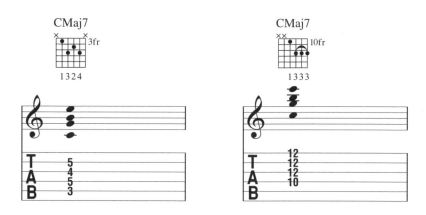

Dominant 7

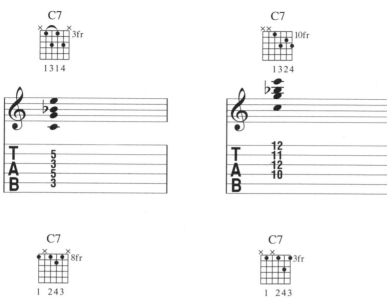

Minor 7

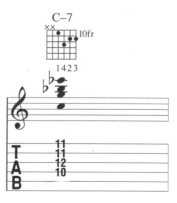

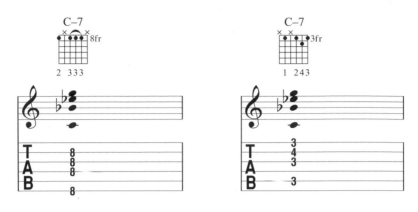

Minor 7♭5

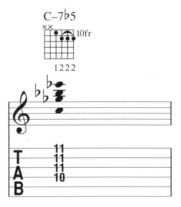

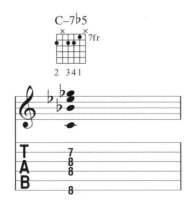

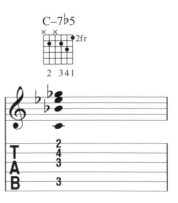

Major 6

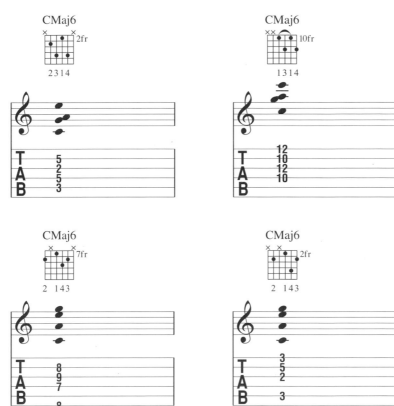

Minor 6

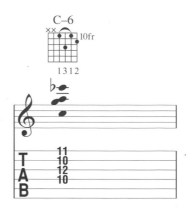

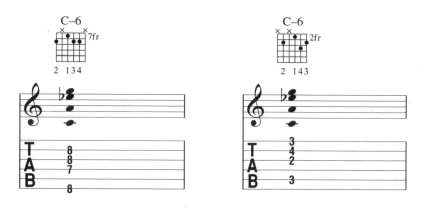

Diminished 7

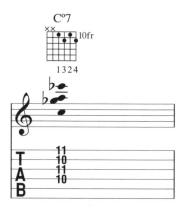

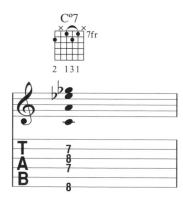
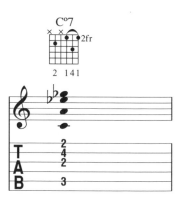

Dominant 9

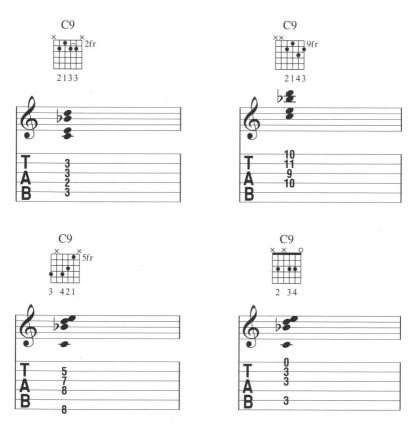

Minor 9

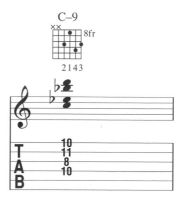

Minor 11

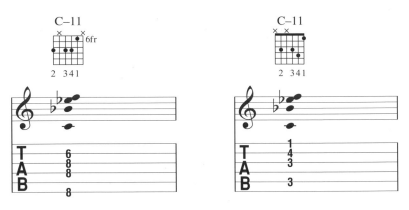

Dominant 13

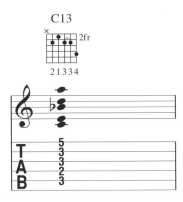

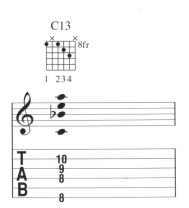

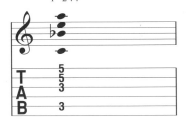

Chapter 2.
Dominant 7th Chords
with Alterations

Dominant 7♭5

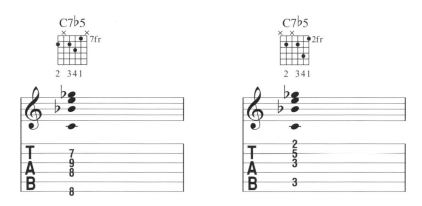

Dominant 7(♯11)

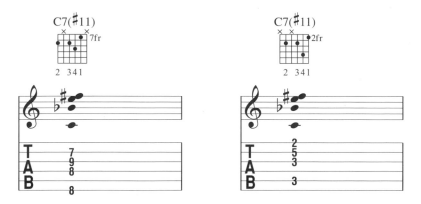

Dominant 7(9), Dominant 7#9

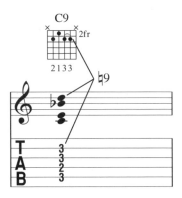

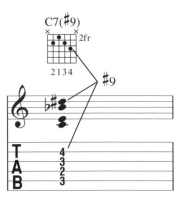

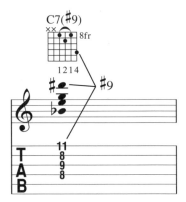

Dominant 7#5

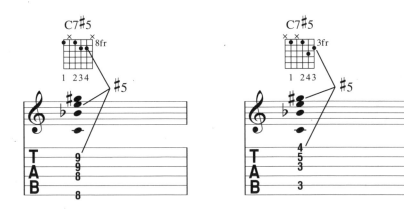

Dominant 7 (♭9, ♭13)

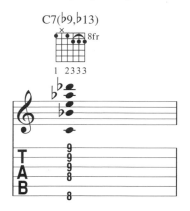

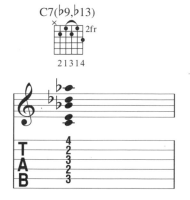

Dominant 7(altered)

7♭5(♭9)

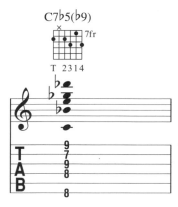

7♭5(♯9)

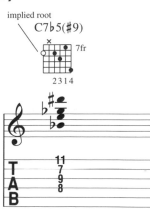

implied root
C7♭5(♯9)

C7♭5(♯9)

7♯5(♭9)

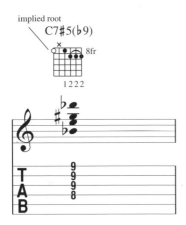

7♯5(♯9)

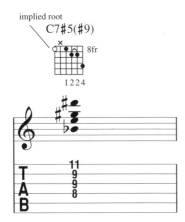

Chapter 3.
Guide Tone Chords

Root 3 7

CMaj7

C7

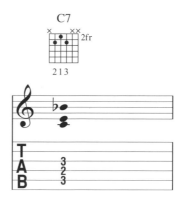

C–7

C–7♭5   (incomplete)

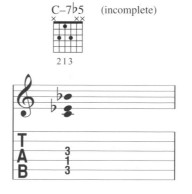

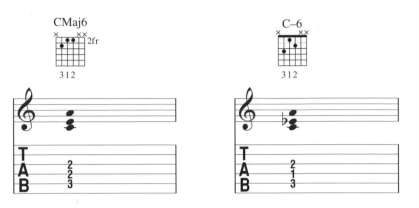

Root 7 3

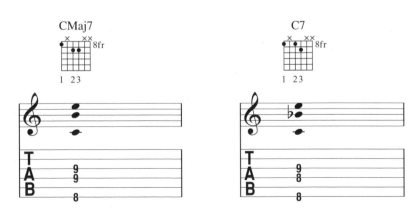

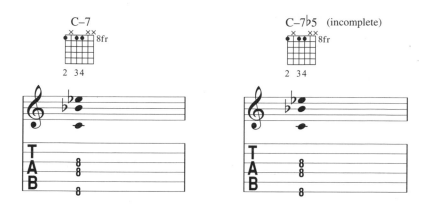

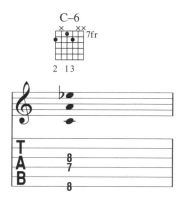

Chapter 4.
Triads over Bass-Note
Voicings: Roots on ⑥ ⑤ ④

V/I

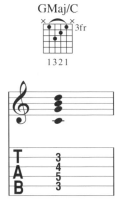

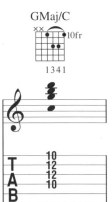

♭VII/I

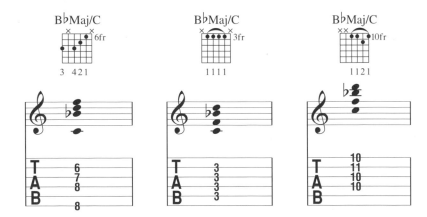

Other Common Voicings

III/I

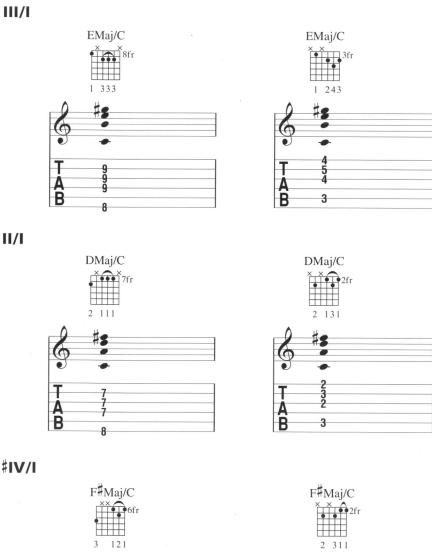

II/I

♯IV/I

VI/I

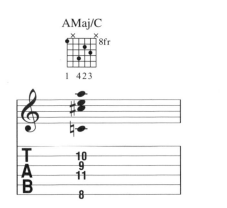

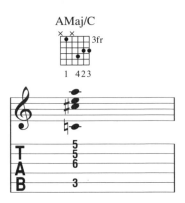

VII/I

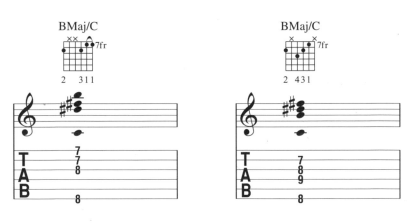

Chapter 5.
Inversions

Major 7

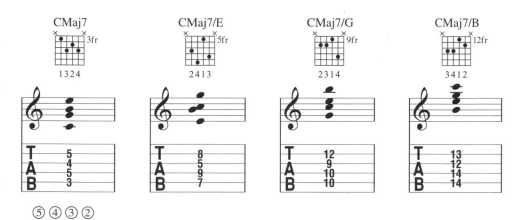

CMaj7   3fr   1324

CMaj7/E   5fr   2413

CMaj7/G   9fr   2314

CMaj7/B   12fr   3412

⑤ ④ ③ ②

CMaj7   8fr   1 342

CMaj7/E   10fr   2 134

CMaj7   8fr   1 342

CMaj7/B   5fr   3 111

CMaj7/G   3 241

⑥ ④ ③ ②

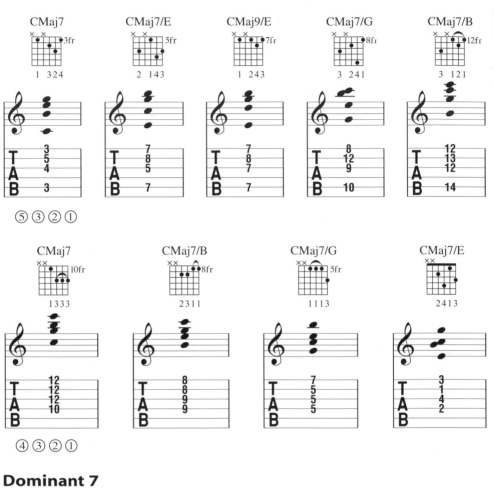

Dominant 7

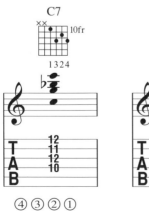

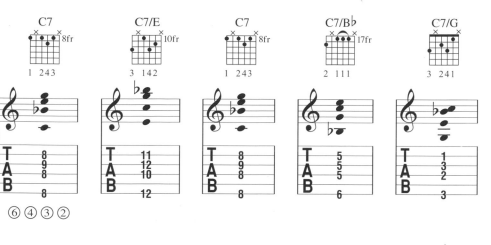

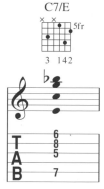

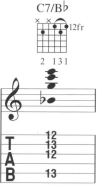

Minor 7

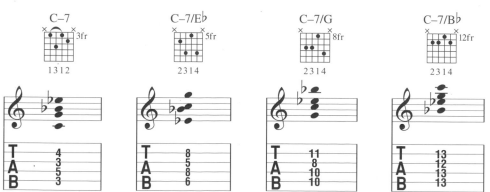

INVERSIONS

22

Minor 7♭5

C–7♭5

C–7♭5/E♭ same as E♭–6

C–7♭5/G♭

C–7♭5/B♭

⑤ ④ ③ ②

C–7♭5

C–7♭5/B♭

C–7♭5/G♭

C–7♭5/E♭ same as E♭–6

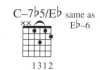

④ ③ ② ①

C–7♭5

C–7♭5/E♭ same as E♭–6

C–7♭5

C–7♭5/B♭

C–7♭5/G♭

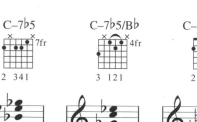

⑥ ④ ③ ②

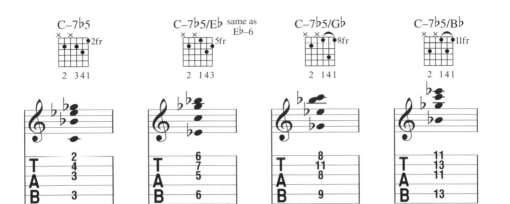

C–7♭5   C–7♭5/E♭ same as E♭–6   C–7♭5/G♭   C–7♭5/B♭

Major 6

CMaj6   CMaj6/E   CMaj6/G   CMaj6/A same as A–7

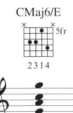

CMaj6   CMaj6/A same as A–7   CMaj6/G   CMaj6/E

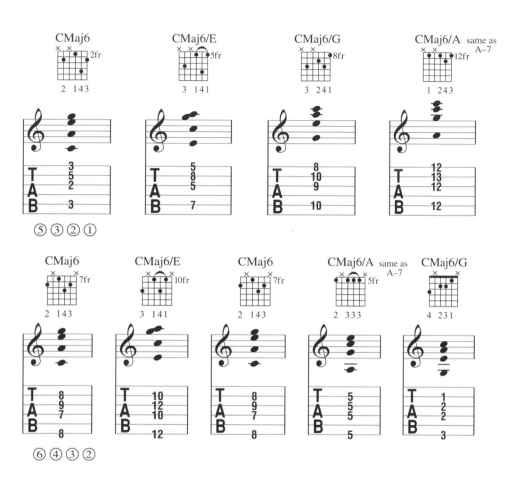

Minor 6

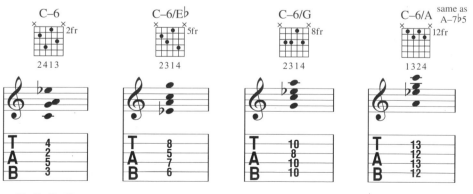

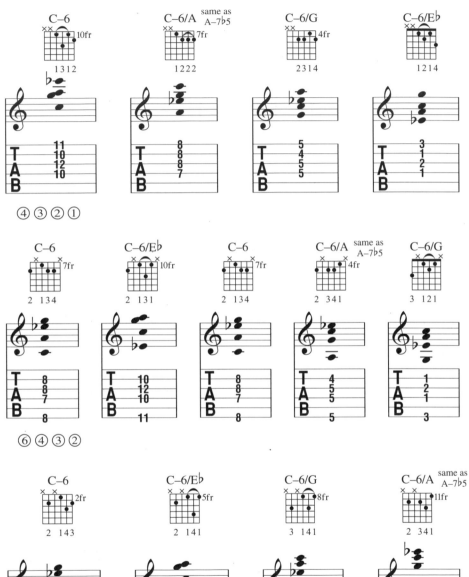

PART II.
EXERCISES

Chapter 6.
Quartal Voicings Exercises

C Dorian Voicings

(for use on C–7 or F7sus4)

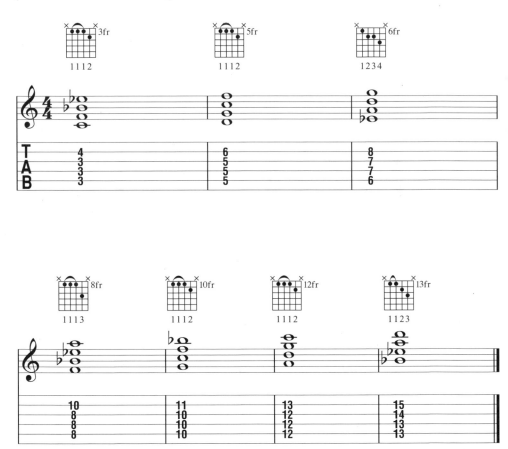

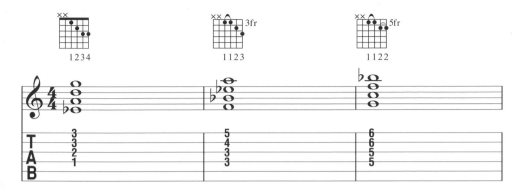

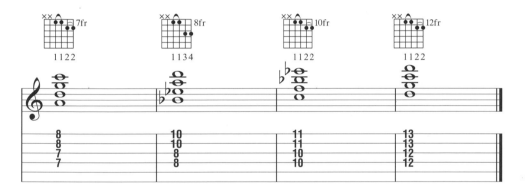

Chapter 7.
Diatonic Exercises

B♭Major on ⑤ ④ ③ ②

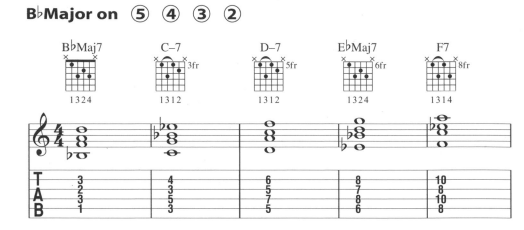

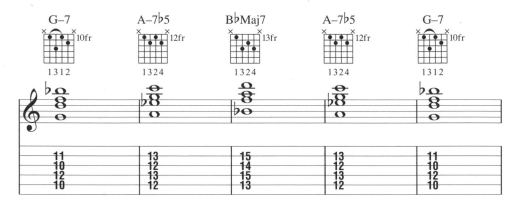

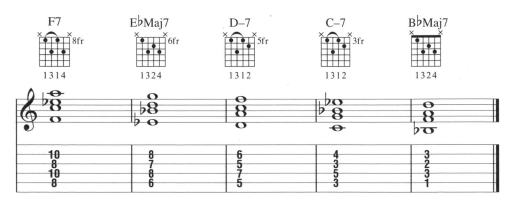

Eb Major on ④ ③ ② ①

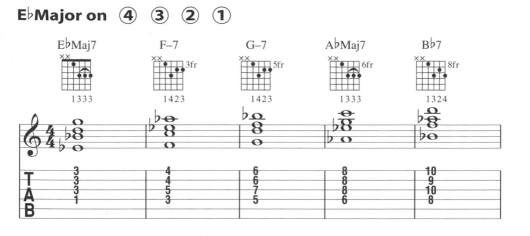

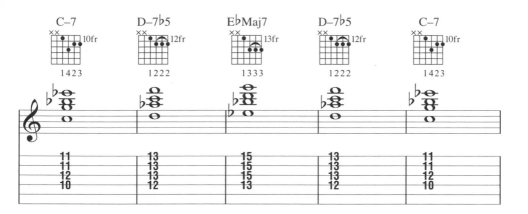

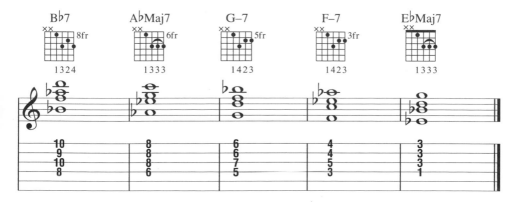

F Major on ⑥ ④ ③ ②

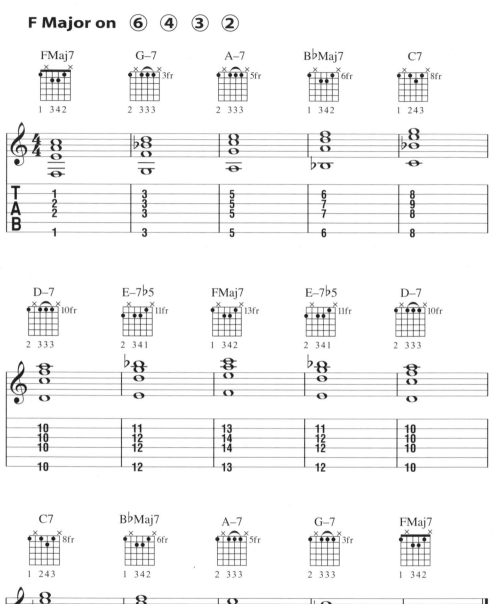

B♭ Major on ⑤ ③ ② ①

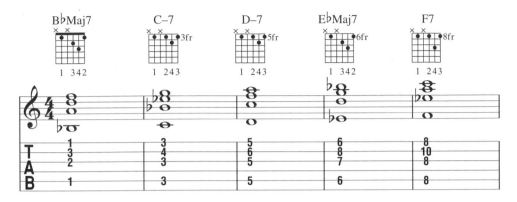

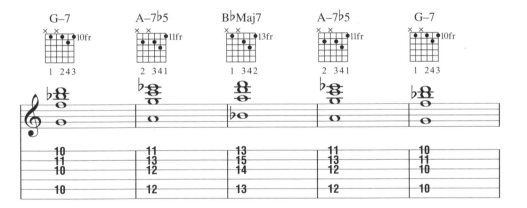

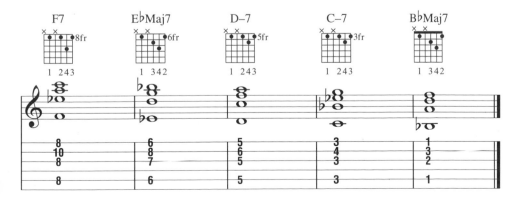

F Harmonic Minor on ⑥ ④ ③ ②

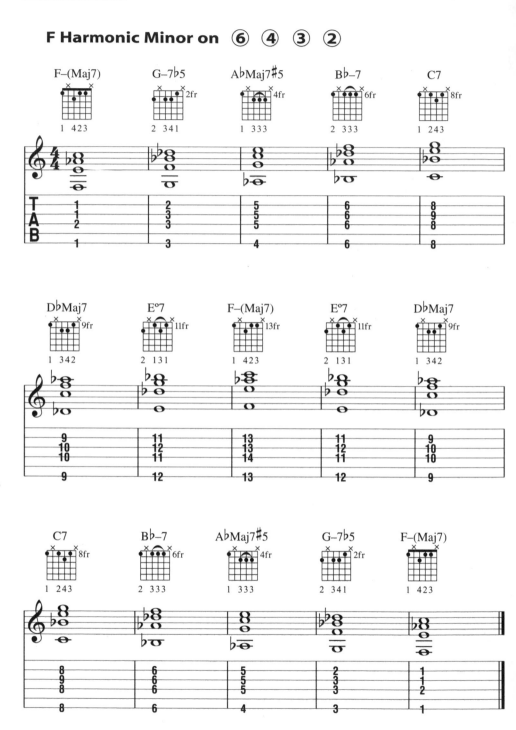

F Melodic Minor on  ⑥ ④ ③ ②

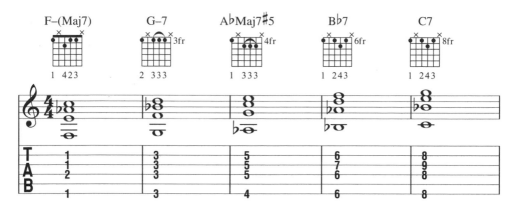

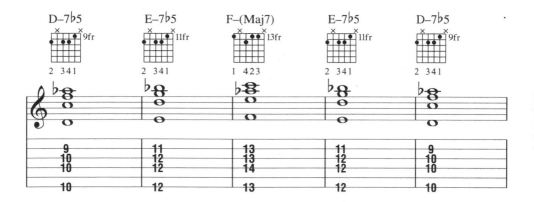

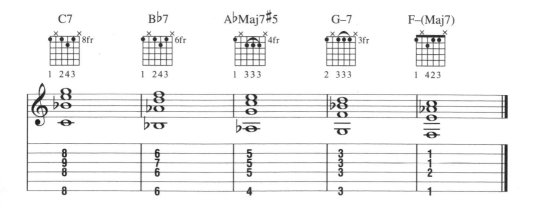

G Major 6 Bebop Scale on ⑥ ④ ③ ②

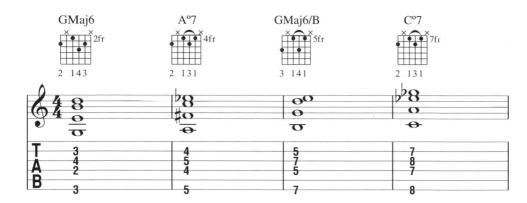

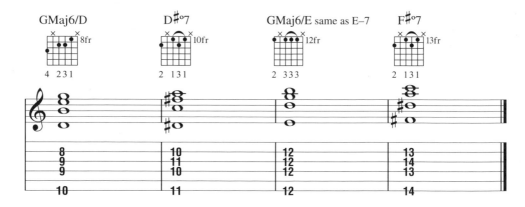

G Minor 6 Bebop Scale on ⑥ ④ ③ ②

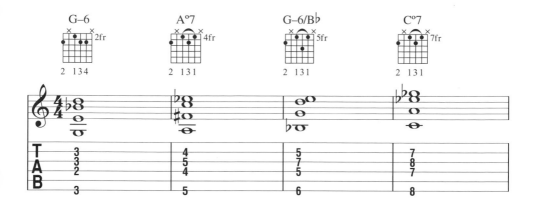

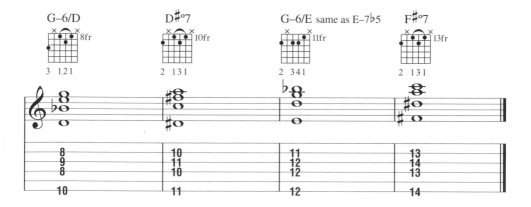

About the Author

Photo by Craig Reed

Rick Peckham is an internationally known jazz guitarist, clinician, composer, and writer. He has performed with George Garzone, Jerry Bergonzi, Mike Gibbs, Hal Crook, Bob Gullotti, John Medeski, and Dave Liebman. His most recent recording, *Left End*, a set of original compositions mixed with collective improvisations, features drummer Jim Black and bassist Tony Scherr and was named one of the best releases of 2005 by *Downbeat* magazine. In addition to extensive work in the U.S., he has led or played on tours of Ireland, Canada, Spain, and Germany. Assistant Chair of the Berklee College of Music Guitar Department, Peckham has been a faculty member since 1986. He is also a prolific and accomplished writer, recently releasing *Modal Voicing Techniques*, a best-selling DVD for Berklee Press, and the online course *Guitar Chords 101* (Berkleemusic.com).

For further information on Rick Peckham, please visit his Web site: www.rickpeckham.com.

Study Guitar Online
with Berklee music
Berkleemusic, the Continuing Education Division of Berklee College of Music, is now offering the world's first online instructor-led guitar courses and programs.
12-Week Online Guitar Courses
Guitar Scales 101
Guitar Chords 101
Jazz Guitar
Rhythm and Groove Guitar
Blues Guitar Workshop
Getting Your Guitar Tone
Classic Rock Guitar Workshop
Recording and Producing for Guitarists
Online Guitar Certificate Programs
Guitar Master Certificate 8-course program
Guitar Styles Professional Certificate 5-course program
Guitar Skills Specialist Certificate 3-course program
Call 1-866-BERKLEE Today
to Speak with a Student Advisor
www.berkleemusic.com
Financial Aid Available * Flexible Schedules * Study with Berklee Faculty

More Fine Publications from Berklee Press